DUNDEE
Things are looking up

Gordon Anderson

Identify Architectural Landmarks in Dundee City Centre

Enter the Competition

The Prize

£1000

DUNDEE
Things are looking up

Published by ECHO (East Coast Hearts Organisation)
PO Box 10187 Dundee DD5 3WF

© Gordon Anderson

Photographs © Peter Anderson

First published in Great Britain 2006

ISBN 10 : 0-9554226-0-4
ISBN 13 : 978-0-9554226-0-7

Printed by Bruce Clark Printers
Marybank Lane, Lochee, Dundee DD2 3DY
Tel: 01382 622724

www.echoscotland.com

What is ECHO?

ECHO (East Coast Hearts Organisation) is the idea of Gordon Anderson, a resident of Dundee who in 2004, suffered aortic problems so severe that consultants at Ninewells Hospital gave his chances of survival as slim. However, their diagnosis and the subsequent excellent surgery performed at Aberdeen Royal Infirmary were life saving. He suffered two strokes during surgery which resulted in the loss of use of his hands but despite that setback, he is so happy to be tramping Scotland's beautiful turf. For that he wants to make you aware of the following:-

People may criticise, that is a human trait but they must also remember, the vast organisation that is the NHS, is in fact run by ordinary people for us, ordinary people. Millionaire or pauper, underneath we are all alike, just ordinary. What we tend to forget or even worse, are never told about, are the extra-ordinary results achieved. Every person in the East of Scotland and beyond, directly or indirectly, already is or will be affected by heart disorders or related diseases. All are, or will be, grateful to every one of these dedicated people who perform such great deeds to cure and prolong life. What we are unaware of is the amount of aftercare people need to get back to leading a full, fruitful and normal life.

It is to this that ECHO is dedicated, the raising of funds to buy essential equipment to aid recovery. People who have suffered a stroke through heart disease and have to relearn skills, or who have had bypass surgery and have to regain a level of fitness, the victims of coronary artery disease, the angina sufferers, the list is large and getting larger.

This book is dedicated to all who got a grumpy wee so'n'so on the road to recovery and without whom this book would not have been possible:

Maureen, Christopher & Peter Anderson and Pamela Martin
Mrs Helen Holmes
Peter & Frances Anderson
Professor Stuart Pringle - Cardiac Unit & Rehab Team - Ninewells Hospital
Mr Robert Jeffrey - Cardiac Surgeon & Intensive Care - Aberdeen Royal Infirmary
Mr Douglas Gentleman - The Brain Injury Unit - Dundee
Occupational Therapy - Kings Cross - Dundee

For help, assistance and advice in producing this book:
Peter Anderson, Gareth Watt, Ian & Lianda Barnes, Dave Mitchell, Gordon Dow
Bruce & Graham of Bruce Clark Printers
The Lord Provost of Dundee - John R Letford

**Very, very special thanks to all the Sponsors & Friends of Echo,
their sponsorship of the photographs made the project a viable proposition.**

Check the website at - www.echoscotland.com

FOREWORD

I am delighted to write a few words as a foreword to this publication.

I first met Gordon Anderson when he was in a life threatening condition and I can only say that I am delighted he survived a major emergency operation and went on to encourage others in this great fundraising effort publishing a book of Dundee photographs.

I am flattered by his recollection of my surgical skills but would emphasise that as in nearly all aspects of surgery and cardiac surgery in particular, it is a team effort, where every member has a critical important role to play if everything is to run smoothly for the benefit of our patients.

Gordon's condition is not common unlike the epidemic of coronary artery disease with which we are all too familiar. I am sure we all know of someone who has sustained a heart attack or suffers from angina. As Scots, we eat too many pies, drink too much alcohol and do not exercise sufficiently. We probably have a genetic predisposition to atherosclerosis, the disease responsible for coronary artery problems and for many strokes. However, with improved prevention, by education and medication, we anticipate that we can conquer this disease. Support of charities through ECHO will help patients who currently suffer from the rampages of atherosclerosis to return to a normal lifestyle.

I should like to record my own personal support for the charities to which he is donating the proceeds of this venture. Please support his efforts.

Robert R Jeffrey
Consultant Cardiothoracic Surgeon
Aberdeen Royal Infirmary

Please enjoy the photographs
and remember,
keep looking up!

1

START LOOKING UP

Just to start this is a fairly easy one, no clue really required even Sandra Gonzalez could get this without too much trouble. Don't think you'll get every photograph this easily and you will not always get a clue. A competition like this is not meant to be simple, if it could be done in a day or two, it wouldn't be worth the effort. There is no desire to be at all devious, it is a case of keeping your eyes open, remember to maintain a sense of scale and in the main, use the visual clues given by the photographs. Happy hunting, don't get a crick in your neck, enjoy your walk, watch the traffic and appreciate how many more bonny bits that could have been taken.

An ecclesiastic Portal?

2

DUNDEE?

The Pictish name for the earliest known settlement was Alec-tum, meaning 'a handsome place' - the name was still being used alongside the modern name, as late as 1607. William the Lion granted the town the status of burgh by royal charter in 1191. His younger brother David, 8th Earl of Huntingdon it is rumoured, is said to have named the town Donum Dei (God's gift) after narrowly escaping death on returning from the Crusades. The name Dundee is more likely to have come from the Gaelic "Dun Dèagh" meaning 'Fort on the Tay'. "Dun" is a common prefix in Scottish place names such as Dunfermline, Dunbar, Dunkeld etc.

Where can you find a wavy dyke? Think for a couple of minutes, then bingo! you've got it!

Are we the only Dundee?

Dundee, Scotland celebrated its 800th anniversary in 1991, and is known now as the

'City of Discovery'

Statistics for comparison are

Dundee, Scotland, UK, population approximately 140,000, area 68 sq km

for the others here is the current list -

Dundee - Kwazulu Natal, South Africa, population 22000, area - rural

Dundee - Parish of Trelawney, Jamaica, population 9500 (est), area - rural

Dundee - Kane County, Illinois USA, population 5500, area 7sq km

Dundee - Monroe County, Michigan USA, population 3500, area 8sq km

Dundee - Polk County, Florida USA, population 3000, area 7sq km

Dundee - Yamhill County, Oregon USA, population 2500, area 5sq km

Dundee - Yates County, New York USA, population 1700, area 3sq km

Dundee - Restigouche County, New Brunswick, Canada, population 900, area 3sq km

Dundee - Delaware County, Iowa USA, population 200, area 1sq km

Dundee - Holmes County, Ohio USA, population 200, area 1sq km

Dundee - Nobles County, Minnesota USA, population 100, area 1sq km

Dundee - Walsh County, North Dakota USA, population 100, area 2sq km

Dundee - New South Wales, Australia, population 70, area 5sq km

4

5

A recognised candidate?

IAIN STEWART MacMILLAN
1938 to 2006
Photographer

Born in Carnoustie, he was educated at the High School of Dundee and started his career as a trainee manager at a jute factory in Dundee. Feeling he could do greater things, he decided at an early stage to change career and instead went to study photography. A man of very great depth and imagination, his name may be relatively unknown but not his internationally recognised work. His signature piece is the famous and many times copied cover of the Beatles' Abbey Road album featuring Lennon, McCartney, Starr and Harrison striding across a zebra crossing.

6

The latin 'Nemo Me Impune Lacessit' means 'No one provokes me with impunity' it is the motto of the Order of the Thistle and is the inscription around a Scottish one pound coin.

This majestic building has seen more uses than most and has wintered the years well.

7

MARMALADE

Dundee has long been associated with marmalade, the oft told story of how this came about begins sometime in the late 1700s when a Spanish ship with a cargo of oranges docked in Dundee harbour to shelter from storms. A grocer by the name of Keiller bought an amount of the cargo cheaply but found it impossible to sell the bitter oranges. He passed the oranges on to his wife who used them, instead of the normal quinces, to make a fruit preserve. The 'marmalade' was extremely popular and the Keiller family went into production. This is almost certainly fiction, it being more likely that in 1797, James Keiller, who was unmarried, opened a factory with his mother Janet to produce "Dundee Marmalade" that is a marmalade containing thick chunks of rind, the recipe for which, probably invented by Janet, being an adaptation of the already well known fruit preserve.

This poor chap has just got a head, should he take a trip to the torso shop?

ROBERT FLEMING 1845 to 1933

Investment banker. Born in Dundee, he saw America as the place to invest the huge profits from the jute industry. He realised the opportunities relating to the great expansion of the USA and in particular he invested in under-valued railway companies. By the time of his death, he had built up the largest investment trust company in the City of London. He gave £155,000 to build the streets around Fleming Gardens in Dundee. His fame is somewhat overshadowed however, by his grandson Ian Fleming, creator of James Bond.

13

FAMOUS DAUGHTER

Born 1964 as Liz Lynch, she won the Dundee Schools Cross-Country Championship in 1976. As Liz McColgan she won a gold medal for the 10,000 metres at the Commonwealth Games in Edinburgh in 1986 then won a silver medal for the same distance in the Olympics in 1988. She then won gold for the 10,000 and bronze for the 3000 in the 1990 Commonwealth Games. Liz also won the London Marathon in 1996. She was named BBC Sports Personality of the Year in 1991 and awarded an MBE in 1992 and retired from top-class athletics in 2001.

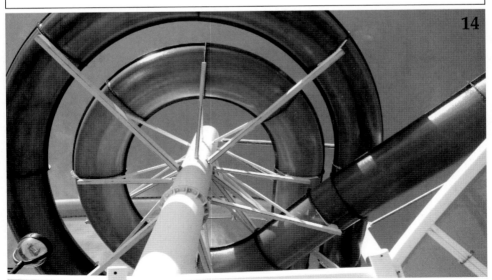

14

15

GRISSEL JAFFRAY

A truly memorable case, when Magistrates of Dundee imposed the extreme penalty of the law along with all the barbarity allowed by the statutes was the martyrdom of Grissel Jaffray in the Seagate in November 1669.

On 11th November of that year, the Privy Council were informed that Jaffray, a prisoner in the Tolbooth of Dundee was accused of "the horrid crime of witchcraft". They issued an order for her trial and the remit to ministers and the Town Council was "If by her own confession, without torture or other indirect means, it should be found that she renounce her baptism, entered into paction with the devil, or otherwise that malefices be legally proven against her, that then and not otherwise they might cause the sentence of death to be executed upon her."

Grissel Jaffray was found guilty of the crime of witchcraft and was burnt at the stake by the people of Dundee.

DUNDEE's ARTIST

James MacIntosh Patrick 1907 to 1988

An etcher and painter celebrated for his finely observed paintings of the Angus landscape and for views in and around Dundee. Born in Dundee, the son of an architect, MacIntosh Patrick studied at the Glasgow School of Art and in Paris.

He began his career as an etcher but when the market for this collapsed in the 1930s he turned towards painting in watercolour and oil and arguably became Scotland's foremost landscape painter. To this day his prints are still top sellers, his best known image is probably the one painted from the top floor studio of his house looking out over Magdalen Green to the Tay Bridge.

16

17

MILLS OBSERVATORY

This is the UK's only full-time public observatory. Built in 1935, it is classically styled and has a distinctive seven metre dome. It houses several fine telescopes, including a Victorian refracting telescope plus a small planetarium and display areas. The Dome is unique, being made from papier maché. On Balgay Hill you will also find the Planet Trail, a series of plaques and standing stones representing the Solar System. These give fascinating facts about each of the planets. Starting from the 'Sun' on the eastern summit of the hill, walk the planet trail until you reach the dwarf planet 'Pluto', which you will find inside the Observatory - located about a mile and a half from the city centre on the summit of Balgay Hill.

Can you be a soldier at this place?

18

THE LESSER SPOTTED FLY?

If you take a walk westward along the Nethergate towards Perth Road there is something you can point out to any fellow traveller. Not many people are aware of it, but if you stop at Sutherlands Gift Shop, look very carefully at the right hand window and you will notice there is a fly embedded in the glass. This little fly went totally un-noticed by the makers of the glass, the glaziers who did the installation and it was only after the window was filled with the many hundreds of items normally on display that the wee beastie was finally spotted. The glazier offered to replace the glass, but it was decided to leave it there rather than go through the whole rigmarole of dressing the window again.

Could be described as Dundee's leaning tower, looking like it could slide off the meadow

FAMOUS SON

Peter Lorimer, born December 14, 1946 in Dundee, a footballer who formed part of the widely admired but universally feared Leeds United team of the late 60's & 70's.

Built for a big retailer of the 1930's and now occupied by a huge retailer of the 21st century.

Robertson's House Furnishers - Willison House - Barrack St - Dundee - 01382 221138

SNIPPETS

- Dundee was second only to London to have its own telephone exchange system •
- Dr George Pirie was among the first in the world to use X-rays in D.R.I. in 1896 •
- In the 1930s, Dundee had more cinemas per head than anywhere else in Europe •
- The Western Club, established in 1869 is thought to be Dundee's oldest club•

THE HIGH SCHOOL OF DUNDEE

More commonly referred to as Dundee High School, it is one of Scotland's leading public schools and the only school in the centre of the city. It has its origins in the Grammar School of Dundee founded by the abbot and monks of Lindores Abbey after they were granted a charter by Gilbert, Bishop of Brechin, in the early 13th century. Their rights were confirmed by a Papal Bull conferred by Pope Gregory IX in February 1239. It is from this Bull that the School's Latin motto "Prestante Domino", translated as "Under the Leadership of God", is taken.

Early scholars included William Wallace, Hector Boece, (see separate story) and James, John & Robert Wedderburn, authors of The Gude and Godlie Ballatis, one of the most important literary works of the Scots Reformation. The School itself was the earliest Reformed School in Scotland, having adopted the new religion in 1554.

The Grammar School merged with two other schools, the English School, founded by the Burgh Council in 1702, and the Dundee Academy, founded 1785 also by the Burgh, to form the Dundee Public Seminaries in 1834 and so moved to a neo-classical building by the architect George Angus, designed as part of the improvements in Dundee. In 1859, a Royal Charter granted by Queen Victoria changed the name of the school to the High School of Dundee.

Recent former pupils include SRU coach Frank Hadden, political journalist and TV presenter Andrew Marr, singer KT Tunstall and Andy Nicol & Tom Smith.

23

24

THE CAIRD HALL

Famous names to play the Caird Hall include Bob Hope, Mario Lanza, Frank Sinatra (he only sold 600 tickets for his first night) the Beatles and Rolling Stones. To further the story, the Beatles reputedly ate in the Deep Sea Restaurant and Frank Sinatra had a drink in the Phoenix Bar.

25

YOONIE in the CENTRE!

Not many cities boast a university right in the city centre but Dundee can. The University of Abertay Dundee was founded in 1888 as the Dundee Technical Institute and later converted into a centrally funded institution with full degree-awarding powers. It was recognised as an "industrial university" by the Scottish Office as early as 1902 and was finally allowed the formal 'university' title in 1994. Since then it has blossomed, adding stunning award winning architecture to its portfolio and is seen today as a forward thinking, state of the art seat of learning, where over 60 different nationalities come to study.

26

MAGGIE'S CENTRE

World renowned architect Frank Gehry opened the Maggie's Centre at Ninewells Hospital, the first building he had designed in the UK. The striking building was named Building of the Year by the Royal Fine Art Commission Trust in 2003 and one of the finest examples of architecture in Scotland by the Royal Institute of British Architects.

29

SHIRLEY ROBERTSON O.B.E.
Olympic sailor

30

Born 1968 and brought up in Dundee, Shirley began her sailing on the River Tay. She gained a degree from Heriot-Watt University. With a 4th place in the Atlanta Olympics in 1996 she then won gold at the Sydney Olympics in 2000 in the Europe class dinghy sailing. She was the first Scottish woman to win Olympic gold since 1912 and Britain's first female Olympic sailing medallist. Shirley reinforced this victory by taking a further gold in the Yngling class in Athens. 'Top Scot' was bestowed on her at the 2004 Glenfiddich Spirit of Scotland Awards.

A bit of a giveaway but a nice blast from the past

31

DICK McTAGGART

Born in 1935 and 1 of 18 children, he was the first British boxer to compete in three Olympic Games - Melbourne 1956, Rome 1960 and Tokyo 1964. He won gold in '56 and bronze in '60. He was Commonwealth Champion in '58, European Champion in '61 and won the British Empire silver medal in '63. He never turned professional, but by winning 610 of his 634 fights he was one of Britain's most successful amateur boxers. Awarded the MBE for boxing, he was one of the first members of the Scottish Sports Hall of Fame in2001.

WILL FYFFE 1885 to 1947

Comedian and singer. Born in Dundee, he began in the music halls but went on to star on stage and film. Perhaps best remembered for his song "I belong to Glasgow". He is buried in Lambhill Cemetery in Glasgow.

LOCAL BITS

32

- More than 2300 people are employed in the creative industries in Tayside, which boasts 200 companies, a healthy turnover contributing to the local economy. Best selling computer games such as Lemmings, F1 2000, Grand Theft Auto, State of Emergency and Denki Blocks were developed by Dundee based companies.
- More than 2200 people are engaged in the life sciences sector in Dundee working in some of the most significant research areas in Europe. Current projects include new drug therapies and treatments for diseases such as cancer, AIDS, sleeping sickness and malaria.
- Dundee Contemporary Arts is recognised as one of the most successful arts projects in the UK. Designed by architect Richard Murphy, it has been a great success since it opened in 1999.

Best hidden kirk in Dundee?

A beautiful seat of learning

- Dundee Repertory Theatre is home to Scotland's only full-time acting ensemble and contemporary dance company. The award-winning theatre stages an all-year-round programme of theatre, comedy, dance and music.
- The multi-award winning museum, Verdant Works, celebrates Dundee's heritage as Juteopolis and depicts the lives of the 50,000 people who worked in the city's jute industry at its height.
- Discovery Point is home to the Royal Research Ship Discovery, in which Captain Scott sailed on his ill-fated 1901/1904 Antarctic Expedition. It boasts a revamped visitor centre and conference facilities, visitors enjoy in-depth and comprehensive, state of the art displays.

34

Beauty and the beasts, classic Victorian it would appear, should outlast the modern counterpart.

How adaptable can buildings be, where hundreds once worked is now home to lots of traffic cones?

35

FAMOUS SON

Brian Denis Cox, CBE - born June 1, 1946 in Dundee, International Scottish actor notable for being the first to play Hannibal Lecter, a role he took in the Michael Mann film Manhunter. In 1995, he appeared in both Rob Roy and Braveheart. Other roles in film include The Ring, X2, Troy and the two Bourne films. He usually plays villains, such as a rogue colonel in X2, the tyrannical Agamemnon in Troy, Pariah Dark in the Danny Phantom television movie Reign Storm. His most famous part to date is probably as the devious CIA official in the Bourne films. He won an Emmy Award in 2001 for his portrayal of Hermann Göering in the television mini series Nuremburg.

Q - How many columns on the Caird Hall?
A - In all there are fourteen, four are square in section two at each end and the middle ten are fluted and circular in section.
Q - How high are the columns?
A - Each column is nine metres and ninety centimetres high or in old money, that is thirty-two feet six inches.

38

DAVID C. THOMSON 1861 to 1954

Born in Dundee, he took charge of the publishing arm of the family firm in 1884 and built it into one of the major forces in British publishing recognised both at home and internationally. The company became D.C. Thomson in 1905 and was the Journalism in Dundee's "Three J's". Newspaper titles include the Courier and Advertiser, the Evening Telegraph and the Sunday Post, which at its height was read by 4 out of 5 of the Scottish population remaining the best-selling newspaper in Scotland. Magazines include the People's Friend and Scot's Magazine. The company is perhaps best known for a vast range of children's comics, including the Wizard in 1922, Hotspur - 1933, Dandy - 1937, Beano - 1938, with characters such as Desperate Dan, Lord Snooty, Korky the Cat and Dennis the Menace. Thomson remained actively involved in running the company until his death. Today more than 200 million newspapers, magazines and comics are produced annually and they employ more than 2000 people. Still based in Dundee, they are the largest major national publishers to retain a presence in Fleet Street. Renowned for their conservatism, in 1992 The Courier and Advertiser was the last daily UK paper to have news, rather than advertisements and notices, on the front page.

39

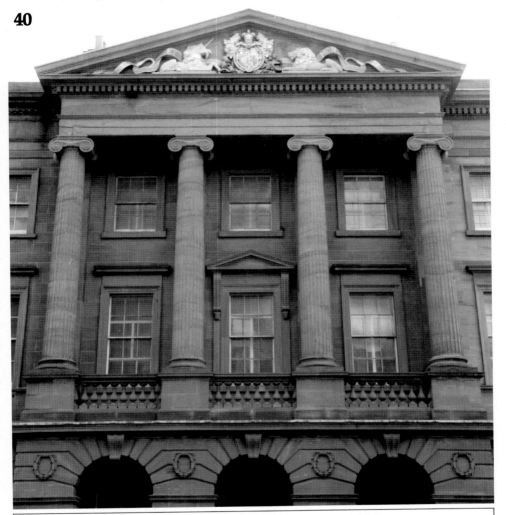

SIR JAMES CAIRD - 1837 to 1916

He was a wealthy Dundee industrialist who famously helped fund Shackleton's famous 1914-16 'Endurance' exhibition.

Dundee's wealth famously came from 3 J's: Jute, Jam and Journalism. James Caird's wealth came from Jute. He was a philanthropist who donated a great deal of wealth, land and buildings to the City of Dundee including the Caird Hall and Caird Park while his sister, Mrs Emma Grace Marryat donated funds for the Marryat Hall.

The James Caird Society, established in 1994 is the only institution that exists to preserve the memory and honour the remarkable feats of discovery in the Antarctic and commends the outstanding qualities of leadership that are associated with the name of Sir Ernest Shackleton 1874 - 1922, especially during the ill-fated but glorious Endurance expedition.

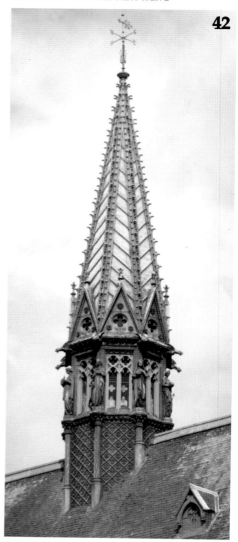

PRESTON WATSON 1880 to 1915
Pioneer of Flight

Born in Dundee, the son of a merchant, Watson experimented with gliders in the Carse of Gowrie, near Errol. He used heavy weights, suspended over the limb of a tree to propel his glider across a field. While wrongly regarded by some to have achieved powered flight before the Wright brothers, it is certain that he managed this feat before 1905 and so became the first Briton to do so and was definitely the first 'Flying Scotsman'. Watson joined the Royal Naval Air Service in 1915 but was sadly killed later that year when the aeroplane he was flying disintegrated in flight and plummeted to earth.

HECTOR BOECE (or BOYCE) 1465 to 1536

Scottish philosopher born in Dundee and where he attended school. Later he studied at the University of Paris and by 1497 had become a professor of philosophy there. In 1500 he was induced to leave Paris for Aberdeen by a generously financed offer to become the first principal of the new university, created at the behest of James IV by the Bishop of Aberdeen. By 1505 regular lectures were taking place at King's College. As intended, Boece was installed as principal and gave lectures on medicine and on divinity. Apart from his work in creating the university, he also wrote books, one of which was the 'History of the Scottish People' up to the accession of James III of Scotland. It was only the second scholarly history of the Scots to be written. By modern standards it is overly patriotic and inaccurate but it was very well received both in Europe and Scotland. The historical account of Macbeth of Scotland flattered the antecedents of Boece's patron, King James IV of Scotland and greatly maligned the real Macbeth. The story as incorporated into Holinshed's Chronicle was used by William Shakespeare as the basis of his play. Boece died in Aberdeen at the age of 71.

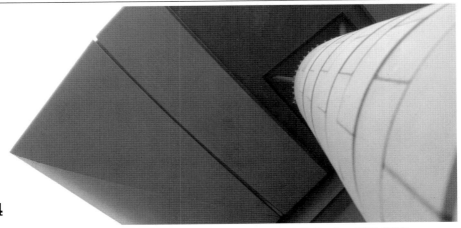

SOME SCOTTISH FACTS

Scotland has the lowest population density in Europe • The furthest you can be from the coast in Scotland is 50 miles. • The first person mentioned in the Bible is a Scot, King James VI • The last battle to be fought on British soil was the Battle of Culloden in 1746 • Scotland is the only country in Europe that the Romans did not fully conquer • The guillotine was used in Scotland 200 years before it was ever used in the France • The shortest scheduled flight in the world, is Westray to Papa in the Orkneys, 1.5 miles in distance and a flight time of 90 seconds • There are more Scots living in Canada than any other country abroad • The greatest distance from North to South of Scotland is 275 miles and the greatest width East to West is 154 miles • There are well over 500 golf courses in Scotland • Edinburgh was the first city in the world to have its own fire service

45

46

CASTLES

Q.   Within the boundaries of Dundee how many castles could you find that are still in existence at present?

A.   **Five** and they are as follows:

1. Broughty Castle
Construction started - circa 1545

2. Dudhope Castle
Construction started - circa 1275

3. Mains Castle
Construction started - circa 1560

4. Powrie Castle
Construction started - circa 1525

5. Claypotts Castle
Construction started - circa 1570

47

48

NINE TRADES

The incorporated trades were formed in the 16th Century and in much the same way as fairtrade works today. The trades were bakers, cordiners (shoemakers), glovers, tailors, bonnet makers, fleshers (butchers), hammermen (metal workers), weavers and dyers. One of the earliest meeting places they used was the Howff Cemetery.

49

Not St. Pauls but if you discover this, it's another to cross off the list.

FACT OR FOLKLORE?

After the siege of Dundee in 1651 when General Monck's men raped, slaughtered and looted, the Town's vast wealth of over 200,000 gold coins was put on ships and the fleet set sail for Leith. The ships foundered on a sandbank and sank, taking the treasure to the bottom of the Tay, somewhere between Broughty Castle and Tayport. Estimated by today's values to be worth over £2 billion, many believe it still lies there, waiting to be found.

Stuart & Pauline Farmer - Friends of ECHO

52

GEORGE DUTCH DAVIDSON
Art Nouveau Painter

Born in Goole, Yorkshire in August 1879 of Dundonian parents, the family returned to Dundee before he was a year old. They lived in Seafield Road and he subsequently went to Hawkhill School and Harris Academy. On leaving school in 1895 he hoped to train as an engineer but he caught influenza, at that time a life threatening infection which necessitated a year of convalescence. He began his painting in 1897 and among his friends were John Duncan, Stuart Carmichael and David Foggie. He studied briefly at Antwerp Academy and travelled to Florence to study the Renaissance painters. He died just a little over three years later in January 1901. To date only thirty-six of his works are known yet it is on this very small portfolio that he is recognised as one of the finest painters of the Art Nouveau period.

53

DUNDEE'S LAST EXECUTION

The last execution to take place in Dundee was in the year 1889 and took place within the walls of the Dundee prison. William Bury, thought by some to be Jack the Ripper, was executed for the crime of murdering his wife. His trial was one of the longest trials in Dundee at the time. The poster (as shown) was placed outside the prison and declared that the sentence of death passed on Bury on the 28th of March was carried out on the 24th of April and includes the certification of his death by the medical officer at the prison. Widely known for his drunkenness, Bury confessed before his death that his plan had been to kill his wife to acquire her money. He carried out the murder, first strangling then stabbing her and placing her body in a trunk. The couple had moved to Dundee from London and acquired lodgings in Princes Street, where the gruesome murder took place.

DECLARATION

THAT THE

SENTENCE OF DEATH

PASSED ON

WILLIAM HENRY BURY

By the Right Honourable LORD YOUNG, one of the LORDS COMMISSIONERS of JUSTICIARY, at DUNDEE, on the 28th day of March 1889

Was carried into effect within the walls of the Prison of Dundee, between the Hours of Eight and Nine o' clock a.m., on the 24th day of April 1889.

We the undersigned, hereby declare that SENTENCE OF DEATH was this day executed on WILLIAM HENRY BURY, in the Prison of Dundee, in our presence. Dated this Twenty fourth day of April, Eighteen hundred and eighty nine years.

JNO.CRAIG, Magistrate.
WM. STEPHENSON, Magistrate.
WILLIAM GEDDES, Governor.
DAVID R. ROBERTSON, Chaplain.
C. TEMPLEMAN, M.B., Police Surgeon.
D. DEWAR, Chief Constable.
JNO. CROLL, Assistant Town Clerk.

CERTIFICATE
OF THE SURGEON OF THE PRISON OF DUNDEE

I, JAMES WILLIAM MILLAR, Surgeon of the Prison of Dundee, hereby certify that I this Day examined he body of WILLIAM HENRY BURY, on whom SENTENCE OF DEATH was this day executed in the Prison of Dundee, and that, on that examination, I found that the said WILLIAM HENRY BURY was dead.
Dated this twenty fourth Day of April, Eighteen hundred and eighty nine years.

J.W.MILLER M.D.,
MED OFFICER, H.M. PRISON, DUNDEE

54

This is far too easy but the light was just right and the photograph was just too good to miss

MARY SLESSOR
1848 to 1915

A mill worker who became a notable missionary in West Africa. With enormous strength of will she unflinchingly took on the authorities to bring genuine benefits to the natives, setting up many schools, hospitals and churches throughout the region. Called 'Great Mother' by the Nigerians, she provided healthcare and education and stamped out barbaric tribal practices such as human sacrifice, ritual rape and the murder of twins.

THOMAS MacLAGAN
1838 to 1903

He was a pharmacologist and doctor born and educated in Dundee. He was medical superintendent at the Royal Infirmary from 1864 to 1866 during which he had to cope with a major fever epidemic and pioneered the use of thermometers.

His most important work however, was research carried out into the anti-rheumatic effects of salicin, a chemical extract from willow bark.

56

57

58

Two distinctly different influences, the first above, borrows heavily on the American desire to reach upward in architectural terms and the second below, their now unfortunate trait in outward growth.

59

JAMES THOMSON
1852 to 1927
Architect and Engineer

60

Thomson was born in Edinburgh where he trained. He joined Dundee Corporation and was involved in the implementation of the City's Improvement Act of 1871. In the year 1906 he was appointed to the post of City Architect and was responsible for various public buildings in the city, most notably the Caird and Marryat Halls, the Blackness and Coldside Libraries in 1909, the Ward Road Museum in 1911 and his revolutionary housing for Council tenants. He proposed a ring road - the Kingsway which was a concept far ahead of its time. He was also the first from a Scottish town to be elected President of the British Institute of Municipal and County Engineers.

61

ROBBIE McINTOSH
Musician 1950 to 1974

Born in Dundee he began his musical career with the R&B group 'The Senate' in the late '60s. He gained fame as drummer in the Average White Band, which formed in 1972, the band quickly moved to the USA where they entered the album charts in 1974. McIntosh died as the result of a heroin overdose at a Hollywood party in September 1974.

PETER NIVEN

National Hunt jockey who has ridden 1000 winners becoming the 6th British jockey to achieve this and the first Scot.

RICKY ROSS
Singer song-writer

Born and brought up in Dundee, Ross was responsible for bringing together the highly successful band Deacon Blue in 1985.

WILLIAM TOPAZ McGONAGALL

62

1830 (est) to 1902

A 'Famous Dundonians' would not be complete without 'our' adopted son. His reputation as "world's worst poet" seems slightly quixotic because now he is read, quoted and enjoyed more than ever, still perhaps though, more for amusement rather than insight.

His parents moved from Ireland so McGonagall was born in Edinburgh around 1830. McGonagall's father was a hand-loom weaver and the family moved around before settling in Dundee. Due to lack of money, William's education lasted only eighteen months but it was enough to get him reading and writing. Although he trained as a weaver like his father, he flirted with a brief career on the stage.

63

As McGonagall himself said, "The most startling incident in my life was when I discovered myself to be a poet, which was in the year 1877." The fact that his audiences were more amused than impressed did not perturb him. His self-belief as a poet was unshakeable and after walking all the way from Dundee to Balmoral in an unsuccessful attempt to drop in to see Queen Victoria, it left him not in the slightest discouraged so he wrote 'An Ode to the Queen in Her Jubilee Year'. McGonagall's poems on the 'Famous Tay Whale' and the 'Tay Bridge Disaster' are perhaps his most famous but he also produced a great many other poems about the people, places and events of his day. His wayward rhymes, unique style and choice of subject still justify the title of worst poet but he is held in great affection.

TAY ROAD BRIDGE

Opened by Queen Elizabeth the Queen Mother on the 18th August 1966, the Tay Road Bridge crosses the Tay estuary linking Newport in north east Fife with the City Centre. Designed by William Fairhurst and built at a cost of nearly £6 million by the Duncan Logan construction company, the bridge measures 2250metres (1.4 miles) long and crosses the Tay 10metres (average) above water level. A 15.5metre (51-feet) high obelisk at the Fife end of the bridge commemorates Willie Logan (1913-66) a director of the construction company, Robert Lyle, former town clerk of Dundee and five men who died while the bridge was being built. If built today, it is estimated the same bridge would cost more than £120 million.

MICKEY MOUSE

In 1946, when Walt Disney became too busy with business projects to continue providing the voice of Mickey Mouse, the job was taken over by Jim MacDonald, a veteran Disney sound and vocal effects man. Born in Dundee in May 1906, he continued to provide the voice of Mickey Mouse for nearly thirty years until he retired in 1974. He is credited with over 30 'Mickey' films as well as continuing to provide sound effects on countless other Disney movies. He died from heart failure at the age of 84 in Glendale, California.

65

Not quite sure what it depicts and only the shadow shows what is the right way up!

A DUNDEE WORTHY

George Mill or 'Bloody Geordie 'as he was known, was one of the Howff gravediggers in the 1840s. Known for his foul mouth, he was suspected of but never caught for grave robbing, a means of supplementing a meagre income by supplying students of medical science with the essential material for dissection, experimentation and study.

66

OOR WULLIE 1936 to ...

An almost legendary cartoon character appearing weekly in the almost as legendary "Sunday Post" This mischievous dungaree-wearing boy is known for uttering "Jings! Crivvens! Help ma Boab!" and was created by Dudley D. Watkins (see below).

DUDLEY D WATKINS
Cartoonist and Illustrator - 1907 to 1969

Born in Manchester, Dudley Dexter Watkins, joined the company of D.C.Thomson in 1925, to draw their cartoon strips. He produced a range of characters for their newspapers and comics including Oor Wullie and The Broons for the Sunday Post in 1936, Desperate Dan and Korky the Cat for the Dandy and Lord Snooty and Biffo the Bear for the Beano. For his loyalty to D.C. Thomson coupled with the level of his success, he was the only artist permitted to sign his work and for which he was paid handsomely.
Following his death, to this day his characters and style are faithfully maintained.

ROBERT STIRLING NEWALL
Scottish Engineer - 1812 to 1889

Born in Dundee, he patented a new type of wire rope in 1840 and established a factory for its manufacture in partnership with Messrs. Liddell and Gordon. He was instrumental in developing substantial improvements to submarine telegraph cables by devising a method involving the use of gutta percha surrounded by strong wires.
The first successful Dover to Calais cable, laid in 1851, was manufactured in Newall's works and approximately half of the Atlantic cable was also manufactured there.

71

HEATHER RIPLEY

Child actress, born in Dundee in 1959. She appeared at the tender age of seven as Jemima in Chitty Chitty Bang Bang - a film still popular to this day. She still lives in Broughty Ferry and is now better known as an active environmental campaigner.

72

SIR ALEXANDER SCRYMGEOUR
Loyalist
c.1254 to 1306

Born in Dundee, Scrymgeour is best known as Royal Standard Bearer, an appointment granted by the the Guardian of the Kingdom, Sir William Wallace 1274 - 1305. Scrymgeour notably carried the standard under Wallace at the Battle of Falkirk in 1298 when the Scottish Army was defeated by Edward I of England. He was created Hereditary Constable of Dundee Castle and granted land at Dudhope on which he built a house later to become Dudhope Castle. After Wallace's death, Scrymgeour continued to support the cause of Scottish Independence and Robert the Bruce (1274 - 1329). He was captured at Methven in1306 and taken to Newcastle-upon-Tyne where he was executed in 1306.

73

74

WINSTON CHURCHILL

From 1908 to 1922, the city's MP, at that time a Liberal. Churchill's conspicuous noble background and his absences from Dundee on cabinet business alienated him from his constituents. The last years of his tenure in Dundee were marked by vitriol from local newspapers. He once described the constituency as "a life seat and cheap and easy beyond all experience". Prevented from actively campaigning in the 1922 election by appendicitis, his wife Clementine spoke for him instead. Churchill was ousted by the Labour candidate E. D. Morel and the Scottish Prohibitionist Edwin Scrymgeour - in Scrymgeour's case, at the sixth attempt. Churchill would later write that he left Dundee "short of an appendix, seat and party". In 1943 he was offered the Freedom of the City - by 16 votes to 15 - but he refused to accept. On being asked by the Council to expand upon his reasons, he said simply: "I have nothing to add to the reply which has already been sent".

75

77

SOME WEE FACTS

Mary Godwin, later to marry the poet Shelley, wrote part of her book 'Frankenstein' in Dundee, reputedly in Peep o' Day Lane • Sir Robert Watson-Watt born in Brechin and educated at Dundee University invented radar, he was also a descendant of James Watt who invented the steam engine • Robert the Bruce was pronounced 'King' at Dundee Castle which stood approximately where the bottom of Castle Street is today.

78

PARTANCRAIG?

We all think of Broughty Ferry as being Dundee's 'beach' but few remember it was originally known as 'Partancraig'. The village was a proudly independent fishing community to the East that was reluctantly incorporated into an expanding City in 1913.

82

WILLIAMINA PATON STEVENS FLEMING
Astronomer
1857 to 1911

Born May 15 in Dundee, she went to public schools in the town and then taught from age fourteen until her marriage to James Fleming in 1877. The couple emigrated to Boston when she was 21. A year later she was abandoned by her husband while pregnant with their only child. To support herself and the baby, 'Mina' obtained work as a maid in the home of Professor Edward Pickering the director of the Harvard Observatory.

Pickering was unhappy with work performed by his male staff and declared angrily that his maid could do a better job. He in fact, hired her in 1881 to do some mathematical calculations at the Observatory. She soon proved more than capable of doing scientific work and devised a system of classifying stars. She used this system, which was later named after her, to successfully catalogue over 10,000 stars in the next nine years. Her duties were expanded and she was put in charge of dozens of young women hired to do mathematical computations. She also edited publications issued by the observatory, the quality of her work so superior that in 1898 Harvard appointed her curator of astronomical photographs. This was the first such appointment ever to be given to a woman.

In 1906 she was the first American woman elected to the Royal Astronomical Society and then in 1910 she published her discovery of "white dwarfs" believed to be stars in their final stage of their existence. Williamina Fleming died suddenly of pneumonia in Boston 1911 at the relatively young age of 54.

83

85

Can you imagine how many stonemasons would be needed and why they were always in demand? Records show it was a very popular trade to be apprenticed into and a skilled mason was a top earner.

MORE WEE FACTS

The Old Steeple is 156 feet high • The Seagate was originally St. Mary's Gate • The Overgate Centre has 28 pieces of sculpture attached to its walls • Joanna Lumley starred at the Rep • Crichton Street is named after the eminent surgeon John Crichton, whose house was demolished to make way for the new thoroughfare that ran down towards the harbour • The McManus Galleries, or the 'Museum' or 'Albert Institute' as known when built was designed by Sir Gilbert Scott and used as a trial run for the building of Glasgow University.

The Staff at The Carphone Warehouse - Murraygate - Dundee

Not too difficult - hint: the one above is a recognisable city centre church and the one below isn't!

93

No rocket science required here, if you don't recognise these two, you left your white stick at home!

94

ALFRED ANDERSON 1896 – 2005
Took part in the 1914 World War Christmas Truce

He left home in October 1914 and joined the Angus and Dundee Battalion of the Black Watch, he thought he was going on an adventure to go and fight the Huns on the Western Front. On December 24th and 25th, 1914 he was billeted in a farmhouse away from the front line, so he did not actually take part in any of the famous football matches that took place between the 'Tommies' and the German soldiers, who also swapped cigarettes and rations. However, he recalled the day and said "I remember the eerie sound of silence. We all went outside the farm buildings and just stood listening. All we'd heard for two months in the trenches was the hissing, cracking and whining of bullets, machine gun fire and sometimes, distant German voices".

In 1916 he was wounded which required recuperation in Britain. After recovering at a hospital in Norfolk he became an infantry instructor and was posted to Ripon, rising to the rank of staff sergeant by the end of the war.

It was during his time as an instructor that he married and after the war, he took his bride back to Scotland to recommence life as a joiner in his father's business.

After his wife died in 1979 he moved to Alyth to be near his youngest daughter. At his death, he was also Scotland's oldest man. He died just a few weeks after featuring in a BBC 1 documentary 'The Last Tommy' which interviewed some of the last surviving First World War British Army veterans. He was survived by 4 children, 10 grandchildren, 18 great-grandchildren, and 2 great-great grandchildren.

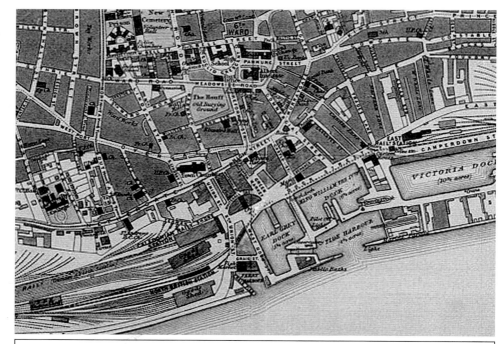

SCOTTISH & PROUD

As if the Scots ever need an excuse to feel proud, but should you forget, or if you happen to be speaking to a foreigner or even someone English, then memorise these few names and facts and spout forth whenever anyone tries to put down the Scots. First there is Alexander Graham Bell who invented the Telephone and John Logie Baird who gave us Television and Janet Keiller who produced Dundee Marmalade. Then there is Charles MacIntosh with the Raincoat, John Paul Jones who founded the American Navy and John Loudon MacAdam without whose Tarmac we would get around much more slowly along with John Dunlop who invented the Pneumatic Tyre, James Chalmers the Postage Stamp, James Watt the Steam Engine and more recently Alexander Fleming discovered Penicillin. Kirkpatrick MacMillan gave us the Bicycle which more of us should get back to using. Alan Pinkerton went to the USA and started the famous Detective Agency and John Campbell travelled and founded the City of Auckland. The Bank of England was founded by William Paterson and John Law despite speaking little French founded the Bank of France. Andrew Fisher was First Prime Minister of Australia and William Smith founded the Boys Brigade, Samuel Craig founded the Russian Navy and Radar was invented by Robert Watson-Watt, Patrick Gordon was Peter the Great's adviser and Charles Cameron designed many buildings in Leningrad during the reign of Catherine the Great. There are more Scots living outside Scotland than inside and Scotland is the only country in the World to have invaded England - twice! More than half the defenders of the Alamo were of Scottish descent, among them Davy Crockett and Jim Bowie it goes on and on but just to finish it off nicely, Scotland is the only country in the world where Coca Cola is not the best selling soft drink, Irn Bru made by the Barrs is still 'Top of the Pops'.

Competition Rules & Guidelines

Closing date - 31st July 2007

DUNDEE 'things are looking up' in the main, is a collection of photographs plus a miscellany of generally accepted facts, some of Dundee's better known sons and daughters with odd snippets and an anecdote or two thrown in for good measure. Principally however, it is about the city centre and it's architecture - good, bad or indifferent; old, middle aged or modern; and where in most cases, how it can all live side by side. Every numbered photograph has been taken specifically for the book and the challenge is to identify as many as possible and then enter the competition where the prize to the winner will be £1000. Every viewpoint is accessible to the public on foot, no buildings were entered and no special effects were used. NOTE - certain buildings may or may not appear more than once and not necessarily from similar angles or viewpoints. NOTE - all pictures are as seen in August/September so allowance should be made for seasonal variations. On the map at the back of the book you will see that the vast majority of streets are named. If a street is not named then no photographs were taken of any buildings in that street. That does not mean however, that viewpoints follow the same rule. Using the grid system on the map it is up to you to work out, using any visual or verbal clues, the spot where the photograph was taken. For example; if you think photograph number 5 was taken at the top of Union Street then using the letter followed by the numbered grids, your answer would be **EE23**. When you have identified as many of the photographs as you can, complete the entry form and return it to the competition address. Write clearly in **BLOCK CAPITALS**. Any entry deemed illegible will be declared null and void. All entries must be on the form taken from the book. Photocopies will not be accepted.

Every effort has been taken to ensure all buildings pictured were not liable for repair, scheduled for demolition or subjects for major alteration. Locations will be checked regularly to ensure no alterations occur. If any subject should change then that photograph will not count for the competition and notification will be put on the website. We will also put up regular postings at < www.echoscotland.com > to keep you updated on progress. The photographs to be identified vary from fairly obvious to "whaur in bloo blazes izzat" so don't worry if you don't get all 100 we don't give away £1000 easily. Anyone spotting over 90 should be in with a good chance. Should there be more than one all correct entry then judges will decide the better entry based on the accuracy of the grid identification. The judges' decision will be final and no correspondence will be entered into. The winner will be notified as soon as a decision is made. Persons directly connected to ECHO or their relations are not permitted to enter the competition. After the closing date, a list of all locations will be posted on the website. Once again sincere thanks for buying the book and participating.

www.echoscotland.com

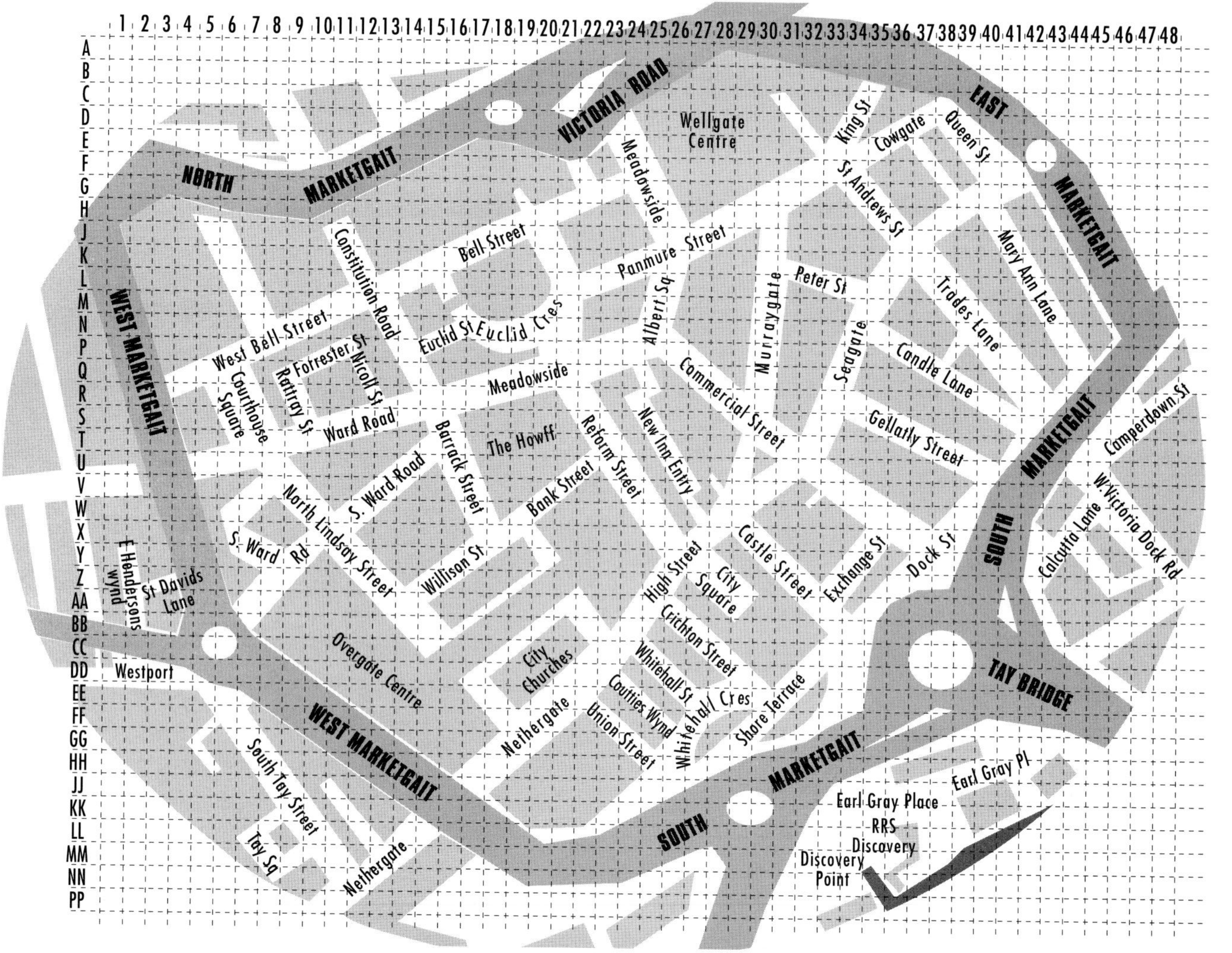

1 2 3 4 5 6 7 8 9 10 11 12 13 14 15 16 17 18 19 20 21 22 23 24 25 26 27 28 29 30 31 32 33 34 35 36 37 38 39 40 41 42 43 44 45 46 47 48
A B C D E F G H J K L M N P Q R S T U V W X Y Z AA BB CC DD EE FF GG HH JJ KK LL MM NN PP
VICTORIA ROAD
NORTH MARKETGAIT
EAST MARKETGAIT
WEST MARKETGAIT
SOUTH MARKETGAIT
TAY BRIDGE
Wellgate Centre
Meadowside
King St
Cowgate
Queen St
St Andrews St
Bell Street
Panmure Street
Constitution Road
Albert Sq
Murraygate
Peter St
Mary Ann Lane
Trades Lane
Seagate
Candle Lane
Gellatly Street
Camperdown St
West Bell Street
Forrester St
Nicoll St
Rattray St
Courthouse Square
Euclid St
Euclid Cres
Meadowside
Commercial Street
Ward Road
The Howff
Barrack Street
Reform Street
New Inn Entry
S. Ward Road
North Lindsay Street
Bank Street
S. Ward Rd
Willison St
High Street
City Square
Castle Street
Exchange St
Dock St
Calcutta Lane
W.Victoria Dock Rd
E Hendersons wynd
St Davids Lane
Westport
Overgate Centre
City Churches
Crichton Street
Whitehall St
Whitehall Cres
Coutties Wynd
Nethergate
Union Street
Shore Terrace
Earl Gray Pl
Earl Gray Place
RRS Discovery
Discovery Point
South Tay Street
Tay Sq
Nethergate

Photo No.	Grid Ref	Photo No.	Grid Ref	Photo No.	Grid Ref	Photo No.	Grid Ref
1		26		51		76	
2		27		52		77	
3		28		53		78	
4		29		54		79	
5		30		55		80	
6		31		56		81	
7		32		57		82	
8		33		58		83	
9		34		59		84	
10		35		60		85	
11		36		61		86	
12		37		62		87	
13		38		63		88	
14		39		64		89	
15		40		65		90	
16		41		66		91	
17		42		67		92	
18		43		68		93	
19		44		69		94	
20		45		70		95	
21		46		71		96	
22		47		72		97	
23		48		73		98	
24		49		74		99	
25		50		75		100	

OFFICIAL ENTRY FORM

Having reached this stage and ready to fill in your answers,
please remember the following points:-
Grid accuracy is most important
Write clearly in ballpoint
Write your name and address in **BLOCK CAPITALS**
send your entry to
ECHO
PO Box 10187
Dundee DD5 3WF

NAME _____

ADDRESS_____

_____

TOWN _____

POST CODE _____

TELEPHONE_____

email _____

Once again, my thanks for not only buying the book and getting this far, but I hope you enjoyed the challenge. It has kept you walking around the streets of Dundee and given exercise to your body and your heart. The battle against heart disease will continue, as will ECHO's efforts to help those who are getting through recovery. I know just how much it can touch upon many people.

I hope that some time in the future you might help further. Send donations (please make cheques payable to 'Echo') to the address above marked for my attention - and once again my sincerest thanks

Gordon Anderson
October 2006